U.S. Citizenship Test Practice (English) 2019 - 2020
100 Civics Questions plus Flashcards, USCIS Vocabulary and More

INSTITUTE *of*
Museumand**Library**
SERVICES

Lakewood Pub

U.S. Citizenship Test Practice (English) 2019 - 2020
100 Civics Questions plus Flashcards,
USCIS Vocabulary and More

ISBN 978-1-936583-65-2
Copyright © 2019 by Lakewood Publishing

Published by Lakewood Publishing
275 E. Hillcrest Ave., #160 Ste. 213
Thousand Oaks, CA 91360

1. Citizenship, United States, America, U.S. 2. naturalization, citizenship 3. immigration, citizenship test, new test
4. English – language 5. United States – civics, government
6. United States – USCIS test October 2018
I. Citizenship, American   II. Title

U.S. Citizenship Test Practice

English 2019 – 2020
100 Civics Questions, plus
Flashcards, USCIS Vocabulary and More

For Civics and Citizenship
www.lakewoodpublishing.com

Learning About the United States: 100 Citizenship Questions, Civics Readings and More for the New U.S. Citizenship Test
ISBN 978-1-936583-57-7
ISBN 978-1-936583-62-1 (ebook)

U.S. Citizenship Test Series: Multilingual

U.S. Citizenship Test Practice (English) 2019 - 2020
100 Civics Questions, plus Flashcards, USCIS Vocabulary and More
ISBN 978-1-936583-65-2

U.S. Citizenship Test Practice (Spanish • English) 2019 - 2020
100 Bilingual Civics Questions (Español • Inglés), plus Flashcards, USCIS Vocabulary and More
ISBN 978-1-936583-66-9
100 Preguntas y Respuestas para el Examen de E.U. Ciudadanía

U.S. Citizenship Test Practice (Chinese – English) 2018 - 2019
100 Bilingual Civics Questions (中文- 英文), plus Flashcards, USCIS Vocabulary, and More
ISBN 978-1-936583-54-6
公民入籍歸化考試的 100 道考題與答案

U.S. Citizenship Test Practice (Korean – English) 2018 - 2019
100 Bilingual Civics Questions (한국어 - 영어), plus Flashcards, USCIS Vocabulary, and More
ISBN 978-1-936583-55-3 미국시민권시험인터뷰질문

U.S. Citizenship Test Practice (Vietnamese – English) 2018 - 2019
100 Bilingual Civics Questions (tiếng Việt - tiếng Anh), plus Flashcards, USCIS Vocabulary, and More
ISBN 978-1-936583-56-0
100 câu hỏi và câu trả lời để chuẩn bị cho kỳ thi quốc tich Mỹ

Also Available

Surviving Disasters: From Earthquakes and Fires to Storms and Terrorism
ISBN 978-1-936583-63-8
ISBN 978-1-936583-64-5 (ebook)

THE ELEMENTS OF STYLE* **18 Essential Rules for Good Writing in English** (*Strunk's original; newly formatted*)
ISBN 978-1-936583-36-2

The Jefferson Bible: What Thomas Jefferson Selected as the Life and Morals of Jesus of Nazareth
ISBN 978-1-936583-21-8
ISBN 978-1-936583-22-5 (hardcover)
ISBN 978-1-936583-27-0 (ebook)

The DASH Diet Solution and 60 Day Weight Loss and Fitness Journal
ISBN 978-1-936583-29-4
ISBN 978-1-936583-28-7 (hardcover)

How-To Guides (in Spanish or English) for Immigrants Living in the United States

A Guide for New Immigrants to the United States: What Everyone Should Know
ISBN 978-1-936583-58-4

Un guía para inmigrantes nuevos a los Estados Unidos: lo que deben saber
ISBN 978-1-936583-59-1

Contents

Are You Eligible for U.S. Citizenship?

Every year, thousands of people from all over the world choose to become citizens of the United States. For many, it is the fulfillment of a dream.

When permanent residents become U.S. citizens, they receive new rights, including being able to vote, to serve on a jury, and to travel abroad with a U.S. passport. U.S. citizemship is a long process, but it is a rewarding one.

In general, to become a naturalized U.S. citizen, you must meet the following requirements:

Be at least 18 years old.

Be able to read, write, and speak basic English.

Have a basic understanding of U.S. history and government (civics).

Be a person of good moral character.

Demonstrate an attachment to the principles and ideals of the U.S. Constitution.

*Be a permanent resident of the U.S. for at least 5 years.

*Demonstrate continuous permanent residence in the United States for at least 5 years.

*Show that you have been physically present in the United States for 30 months.

*Show that you have lived for at least 3 months in the state or USCIS district where you apply.

*This requirement may change if you are married to a U.S. citizen.
www.uscis.gov

Preparing for Your Citizenship Interview

United States' citizenship can give you many new opportunities, but it is not a quick process. It usually takes over ten years to become a naturalized U.S. citizen.

The 4 Parts of the Citizenship Interview

The USCIS (United States Citizenship and Immigration Services) is responsible for processing citizenship applications. A USCIS officer (interviewer) will ask you to do four things during your citizenship (naturalization) interview:

1. **Speak and Understand Basic English**. The USCIS officer will ask you questions about your N-400 citizenship application form. These will be questions about your life, work, family and your reasons for becoming a citizen. The officer will also ask about any problems with the information on your application.

He will also ask questions to be sure that you have been honest on your application, and that you are qualified to become an American citizen.

2. **Read English**. The USCIS officer will ask you to read 1 out of 3 sentences correctly in English. The USCIS does not tell which sentences they will use for this test. But they have published a list of words you should be able to read. This USCIS reading vocabulary list begins on page 71.

3. **Write English**. The USCIS officer will also ask you to write 1 out of 3 sentences correctly in English. He will read a sentence to you, then you will write it down. The USCIS does not tell which sentences the USCIS officer will use. But they do list the vocabulary words that USCIS wants you to be able to write.

The USCIS-recommended writing vocabulary list begins on page 75.

4. **Know U.S. Civics.** You will also be asked questions about U.S history and government (also called "civics"). All 100 USCIS civics questions and answers are listed in this book, beginning on page 15. If you are over 65 years old and been a Permanent Resident of the U.S. for 20 years or more, you only need to study 20 of these 100 questions. Throughout this book, these 20 questions have been marked with an asterisk (*).

Flashcards. To make all 100 questions and answers easier to practice and learn, they are also formatted as flashcards that you can cut from this book and use to quiz yourself. These flashcards begin on page 86.

There are 100 civics questions on the USCIS list. You will be asked to answer up to 10 of these 100 questions in your citizenship interview. If you answer 6 questions correctly, you will pass the civics test.

The civics questions and answers will all be given orally. You will not be asked to read or write any of the civics answers.

If you do not pass one part of the test, you can take that part again on a different day. You do not have to retake the entire test, only the part that you did not pass.

Bilingual Books Available

The four other books in this *US Citizenship Test Practice* series all have bilingual civics questions. The questions and answers are in Spanish, Chinese, Korean or Vietnamese on one page and the same questions and answers are in English on the opposite page.

If you have difficulty understanding questions using English only, the unique bilingual formatting of these books can be very helpful. Reading in English and also in your native language when you need it, can make it easier to understand and memorize the answers in English.

All five of Lakewood Publishing's *U.S. Citizenship Test Practice* books mark these questions with an asterisk (*) and list these 20 questions separately. This makes these 20 civics questions easier to study for older Permanent Residents.

Other Reference Materials

The civics questions and answers that begin on page 15 are the only information that you need to know for the civics test.

However, if you would like to know more about any of these questions, there are longer readings that explain each answer in more detail in Lakewood Publishing's, *Learning About the United States: 100 Citizenship Questions, Civics Readings and More for the New U.S. Citizenship Test.*

These longer readings are not part of the USCIS citizenship test. But reading more detailed answers can help you understand why each of the 100 civics questions is important for Americans to know. The readings are also a good way to improve your understanding of civics and to build your English vocabulary in history, geography and government.

Learning About the United States also includes new "bonus readings" about famous Americans, including Sonia Sotomayor, Chief Joseph, Harriet Tubman and Fazlur Rahman Khan.

Becoming a U.S. citizen can be a wonderful, life-changing experience. We encourage you on your journey to citizenship and look forward to welcoming you as a new American citizen.

Introduction to the Civics Test

The current 100 civics (history and government) questions and answers for the USCIS naturalization test are included in the following section.

The civics test is an oral test and the USCIS interviewer will ask you, the applicant, up to 10 of the 100 civics questions. You must answer 6 out of these 10 questions correctly to pass the civics portion of the naturalization test. The other parts of the test (reading, writing and speaking English) are scored separately. If you do not pass one part, you can retake that part of the test on a different day.

Note: If you are 65 years old or older and have been a legal permanent resident of the United States for 20 or more years, you may be able to study the 20 questions that are marked with an asterisk (*) and are also in their own section, beginning on page 43.

This book is current as of publication, and no changes are expected before 2021. However, sometimes there are changes because of new political appointments or resignations. Ask yuur local librarian if there have been any unexpected changes to your representative or senator, or to any of the national officials listed here.

Although USCIS knows that there may be other correct answers to the 100 civics questions, you should give the answers that USCIS uses. They are the ones used in this book.

100 Civics Questions and Answers
(USCIS)

Important Note: Some of the citizenship questions list more than one correct answer. Read the directions carefully. If the question does not ask for more than one answer, then you only need to know one of the answers listed for the citizenship test.

American Government

A: Principles of American Democracy

1. What is the supreme law of the land?

    the Constitution

2. What does the Constitution do? (All answers below are correct. Know <u>one</u> for the test.)

    - sets up the government
    - defines the government
    - protects basic rights of Americans

3. The idea of self-government is in the first three words of the Constitution. What are these words?

    We the People

4. What is an amendment? (Know <u>one</u> way to say it.)

    - a change (to the Constitution)
    - an addition (to the Constitution)

5. What do we call the first ten amendments to the Constitution?

    The Bill of Rights

*6. What is <u>one</u> right or freedom from the First Amendment?

    - speech
    - religion
    - assembly
    - press
    - petition the government

7. How many amendments does the Constitution have?

    twenty-seven (27)

8. What did the Declaration of Independence do? (Know <u>one</u> answer for the citizenship test.)

    - announced our independence (from Great Britain)
    - declared our independence (from Great Britain)
    - said that the United States is free (from Great Britain)

16

9. What are <u>two</u> rights in the Declaration of Independence?

   - life
   - liberty
   - pursuit of happiness

10. What is freedom of religion?

   You can practice any religion, or not practice (have) a religion.

*11. What is the economic system in the United States?

   - capitalist economy
   - market economy

12. What is the "rule of law"?
    (Know <u>one</u> of these answers for the test.)

   - Everyone must follow the law.
   - Leaders must obey the law.
   - Government must obey the law.
   - No one is above the law.

B: System of Government

*13. Name <u>one</u> branch or part of the government.

- legislative branch (Congress)
- executive branch (President)
- judicial branch (the courts)

14. What stops one branch of government from becoming too powerful? (There are two ways to say it. Know one).

- checks and balances
- separation of powers

15. Who is in charge of the executive branch?

the President

16. Who makes federal laws?
(Know <u>one</u> way to say it. All are correct.)

- Congress
- Senate and House (of Representatives)
- (U.S. or national) legislature

*17. What are the two parts of the U.S. Congress?

the Senate and House (of Representatives)

18. How many U.S. senators are there?

    one hundred (100)

19. We elect a U.S. senator for how many years?

    six (6)

*20. Who is one of your state's two U.S. senators now?

My senator is: _____

▪ Answers will be different for each state. Check the internet **www.senate.gov** for the current names in your state. You can also ask at your local library.

[District of Columbia residents and residents of U.S. territories should answer that D.C. (or the territory where the applicant lives) has no U.S. senators.]

21. The House of Representatives has how many voting members?

    four hundred thirty-five (435)

22. We elect a U.S. representative for how many years?

    two (2)

23. Name your U.S. representative

My representative is _____.
▪ Answers will be different for each district. See the website: **www.house.gov** for your current representative or ask your local librarian.

[Residents of territories with non-voting Delegates or Resident Commissioners may provide the name of that Delegate or Commissioner. Also acceptable is any statement that the territory has no (voting) representatives in Congress.]

24. **Who does a U.S. senator represent?**

all the people of the state

25. **Why do some states have more representatives than other states? (Know one way to say it.)**

- (because of) the state's population
- (because) they have more people
- (because) some states have more people

26. **We elect a President for how many years?**

four (4)

*27. **In what month do we vote for President?**

November

*28. What is the name of the President of the United States now? (Either is correct.)

    - Trump
    - Donald Trump

Official White House Photo
President Donald Trump

29. What is the name of the Vice President of the United States now? (Either is correct)

    - Pence
    - Mike Pence

Official White House Photo
Vice President Mike Pence

30. If the President can no longer serve, who becomes President?

the Vice President

31. If both the President and the Vice President can no longer serve, who becomes President?

the Speaker of the House

32. Who is the Commander in Chief of the military?

the President

33. Who signs bills to become laws?

the President

34. Who vetoes bills?

the President

35. What does the President's Cabinet do?

- It advises the President

36. What are <u>two</u> Cabinet-level positions?

- Vice President
- Attorney General
- Secretary of Agriculture
- Secretary of Commerce
- Secretary of Defense
- Secretary of Education
- Secretary of Energy
- Secretary of Health and Human Services
- Secretary of Homeland Security
- Secretary of Housing and Urban
     Development
- Secretary of the Interior
- Secretary of Labor
- Secretary of State
- Secretary of Transportation
- Secretary of the Treasury
- Secretary of Veterans Affairs

37. What does the judicial branch do?

- reviews laws
- explains laws
- resolves disputes (disagreements)
- decides if a law goes against the Constitution

38. What is the highest court in the United States?

the Supreme Court

39. How many justices are on the Supreme Court?

> nine (9)

40. Who is the Chief Justice of the United States now?

> - John Roberts

41. Under our Constitution, some powers belong to the federal government. What is <u>one</u> power of the federal government?

> - to print money
> - to declare war
> - to create an army
> - to make treaties

42. Under our Constitution, some powers belong to the states. What is <u>one</u> power of the states?

> - provide schooling and education
> - provide protection (police)
> - provide safety (fire departments)
> - give a driver's license
> - approve zoning and land use

43. Who is the governor of your state now?
The governor is _____.

> ▪ Answers will be different for each state. [District of Columbia residents should answer that D.C. does not have a governor.]

*44. What is the capital of your state?

The States and the State Capitals

Alabama - Montgomery
Alaska - Juneau
Arizona - Phoenix
Arkansas - Little Rock
California - Sacramento
Colorado - Denver
Connecticut - Hartford
Delaware - Dover
Florida - Tallahassee
Georgia - Atlanta
Hawaii - Honolulu
Idaho - Boise
Illinois - Springfield
Indiana - Indianapolis
Iowa - Des Moines
Kansas - Topeka
Kentucky - Frankfort
Louisiana - Baton Rouge
Maine - Augusta
Maryland - Annapolis
Massachusetts - Boston
Michigan - Lansing
Minnesota - St. Paul
Mississippi - Jackson
Missouri - Jefferson City

Montana - Helena
Nebraska - Lincoln
Nevada - Carson City
New Hampshire - Concord
New Jersey - Trenton
New Mexico - Santa Fe
New York - Albany
North Carolina - Raleigh
North Dakota - Bismarck
Ohio - Columbus
Oklahoma - Oklahoma City
Oregon - Salem
Pennsylvania - Harrisburg
Rhode Island - Providence
South Carolina - Columbia
South Dakota - Pierre
Tennessee - Nashville
Texas - Austin
Utah - Salt Lake City
Vermont - Montpelier
Virginia - Richmond
Washington - Olympia
West Virginia - Charleston
Wisconsin - Madison
Wyoming - Cheyenne

[People who live in the District of Columbia should answer that D.C. is not a state and does not have a capital. Residents of U.S. territories should name the capital of the territory.]

*45. What are the two major political parties in the United States?

Democratic and Republican

46. What is the political party of the President now?

Republican (Party)

47. What is the name of the Speaker of the House of Representatives now?

Nancy Pelosi

Nancy Pelosi, Official Portrait
Democratic Congresswoman, California
Speaker of the House

C: Rights and Responsibilities

48. There are four amendments to the Constitution about who can vote. Describe one of them.

- Citizens eighteen (18) and older (can vote).
- You don't have to pay (a poll tax) to vote.
- Any adult citizen can vote.
- A male citizen of any race (can vote).

*49. What is one responsibility that is only for United States citizens?

- serve on a jury;
- vote in a federal election

50. Name one right only for United States citizens.

- vote in a federal election
- run for federal office

51. What are <u>two</u> rights of everyone living in the United States?

- freedom of expression
- freedom of speech
- freedom of assembly
- freedom to petition the government
- freedom of worship
- the right to bear arms

52. What do we show loyalty to when we say the Pledge of Allegiance? (Know one way to say it.)

- the United States
- the flag

53. What is <u>one</u> promise you make when you become a United States citizen?

- to give up loyalty to other countries
- to defend the Constitution and laws of the United States
- to obey the laws of the United States
- to serve in the U.S. military (if needed)
- to serve (do important work for) the nation
- to be loyal to the United States

*54. How old do citizens have to be to vote for President?

eighteen (18)

55. What are two ways that Americans can participate in their democracy?

- vote
- join a political party
- help with a campaign
- join a civic group
- join a community group
- give an elected official your opinion on an issue
- call Senators and Representatives
- publicly support or oppose an issue or policy
- run for office write to a newspaper

*56. When is the last day you can send in federal income tax forms?

April 15

57. When must all men register for the Selective Service?

- at age eighteen (18)
- between eighteen (18) and twenty-six (26)

The Selective Service

American History

A: Colonial Period and Independence

58. What is <u>one</u> reason colonists came to America?

- freedom
- political liberty
- religious freedom
- economic opportunity
- practice their religion
- escape persecution

59. Who lived in America before the Europeans arrived? (Know one way to say it.)

    - American Indians
    - Native Americans

60. What group of people was taken to America and sold as slaves? (Know one way to say it.)

    - Africans
    - people from Africa

61. Why did the colonists fight the British? (Know one answer)

    - because of high taxes ("taxation without representation")
    - because the British army stayed in their houses (boarding, quartering)
    - because they didn't have self-government

62. Who wrote the Declaration of Independence?

    (Thomas) Jefferson

63. When was the Declaration of Independence adopted?

    July 4, 1776

64. There were 13 original states. Name <u>three</u>.

Connecticut   New York
Delaware   North Carolina
Georgia   Pennsylvania
Maryland   Rhode Island
Massachusetts   South Carolina
New Hampshire   Virginia
New Jersey

65. **What happened at the Constitutional Convention? (Know one way to say it.)**

- The Constitution was written.
- The Founding Fathers wrote the Constitution.

66. **When was the Constitution written?**

1787

67. **The Federalist Papers supported the passage of the U.S. Constitution. Name <u>one</u> of the writers.**

- (James) Madison
- (Alexander) Hamilton
- (John) Jay
- Publius

68. What is <u>one</u> thing Benjamin Franklin is famous for?

- U.S. diplomat
- oldest member of the Constitutional Convention
- first Postmaster General of the United States
- writer of "Poor Richard's Almanac"
- started the first free libraries

69. Who is the "Father of Our Country"?

(George) Washington

*70. Who was the first President?

(George) Washington

George Washington,
the First U.S. President

B: The U.S. in the 1800s

71. What territory did the United States buy from France in 1803?

- the Louisiana Territory
- Louisiana

32

72. Name <u>one</u> war fought by the United States in the 1800s.

- War of 1812
- Mexican-American War
- Civil War
- Spanish-American War

73. Name the U.S. war between the North and the South. (Both are correct ways to say the name of this war. Know one way to say it.)

- the Civil War
- the War between the States

74. Name <u>one</u> problem that led to the Civil War.

- slavery
- economic reasons
- states' rights

*75. What was <u>one</u> important thing that Abraham Lincoln did?

-freed the slaves (Emancipation Proclamation)
-saved (or preserved) the Union
-led the United States during the Civil War

Abraham Lincoln,
President during the Civil War

76. What did the Emancipation Proclamation do?

> -freed the slaves
> -freed slaves in the Confederacy
> -freed slaves in the Confederate states
> -freed slaves in most Southern states

77. What did Susan B. Anthony do?

> -fought for women's rights
> -fought for civil rights

C: Recent American History and Other Important Historical Information

*78. Name <u>one</u> war fought by the United States in the 1900s.

> -World War I
> -World War II
> -Korean War
> -Vietnam War
> -(Persian) Gulf War

79. Who was President during World War I?

> (Woodrow) Wilson

80. Who was President during the Great Depression and World War II?

> (Franklin) Roosevelt

81. Who did the United States fight in World War II?

    Japan, Germany, and Italy

82. Before he was President, Eisenhower was a general. Which war was he in?

    World War II

83. During the Cold War, what was the main concern of the United States?

    Communism

84. What movement tried to end racial discrimination?

    civil rights (movement)

*85. What did Martin Luther King, Jr. do?

    -fought for civil rights
    -worked for equality for all Americans

86. What major event happened on September 11, 2001, in the United States?

   -Terrorists attacked the United States.

87. Name **one** American Indian tribe in the United States.

   [USCIS officers will have a list of federally recognized American Indian tribes.]

Apache	Inuit
Arawak	Iroquois
Blackfeet	Lakota
Cherokee	Mohegan
Cheyenne	Navajo
Chippewa	Oneida
Choctaw	Pueblo
Creek	Seminole
Crow	Shawnee
Hopi	Sioux
Huron	Teton

Integrated Civics

A: Geography

88. Name **one** of the two longest rivers in the United States.

   - Mississippi (River)
   - Missouri (River)

89. What ocean is on the West Coast of the United States?

Pacific (Ocean)

90. What ocean is on the East Coast of the United States?

Atlantic (Ocean)

91. Name one U.S. territory.

- Puerto Rico
- U.S. Virgin Islands
- American Samoa
- Northern Mariana Islands
- Guam

92. Name one state that borders Canada.

Alaska
Idaho
Maine
Michigan
Minnesota
Montana
New Hampshire

New York
North Dakota
Ohio
Pennsylvania
Vermont
Washington

93. Name one state that borders Mexico.

- California
- Arizona

- New Mexico
- Texas

*94. **What is the capital of the United States?**

Washington, D.C.

*95. **Where is the Statue of Liberty? (These both mean the same place. Know one way to say it.)**

- New York (Harbor)
- Liberty Island

[Also acceptable are "New Jersey", "near New York City", or "on the Hudson (River)".]

The Statue of Liberty

B: Symbols

96. **Why does the flag have 13 stripes?**

- because there were 13 original colonies
- because the stripes represent the original colonies

*97. **Why does the flag have 50 stars?**

- because there is one star for each state
- because each star represents a state
- because there are 50 states

98. What is the name of the national anthem?

The Star-Spangled Banner

C: Holidays

*99. When do we celebrate Independence Day?

July 4

100. Name <u>two</u> national U.S. holidays.

- New Year's Day

- Martin Luther King, Jr. Day

- Presidents' Day

- Memorial Day

- Independence Day

- Labor Day

- Columbus Day

- Veterans Day

- Thanksgiving

- Christmas

"65/20"
The 20 Civics Questions
for People 65 and older

65/20

20 Civics Questions
If You're 65 or Older

*If you are 65 years old or older AND have been a legal permanent resident of the United States for 20 or more years, you only need to know the questions that have been marked with an asterisk in the previous section.(*) They are also listed below, Questions: #6, 11, 13, 17, 20, 27, 28, 44, 45, 49, 54, 56, 70, 75, 78, 85, 94, 95, 97, 99. You only need to know one of the answers listed, unless the question asks for more.

*6. What is one right or freedom from the First Amendment?

- speech
- religion
- assembly
- press
- petition the government

*11.   What is the economic system in the United States?

- capitalist economy
- market economy

*13.   Name one branch or part of the government.

- Legislative branch (Congress)
- Executive branch (President)
- Judicial branch (the courts)

*17. **What are the two parts of the U.S. Congress?**

the Senate and House (of Representatives)

*20. **Who is one of your state's two U.S. senators?**

My senator is _____
Answers will be different for each state. Look online or ask at your local library.

[District of Columbia residents and residents of U.S. territories should answer that D.C. (or the territory where the applicant lives) has no U.S. Senators.]

*27. **In what month do we vote for President?**

November

*28. **What is the name of the President of the United States now?**

- Trump
- Donald Trump

*44. **What is the capital of your state?**

Answers will be different by state. See page 25

[District of Columbia residents should answer that D.C. is not a state and does not have a capital. Residents of U.S. territories should name the capital of the territory.]

*45. **What are the two major political parties in the United States?**

Democratic and Republican

*49. **What is one responsibility that is only for United States citizens?**

- serve on a jury
- vote in a federal election
- the flag

*54. **How old do citizens have to be to vote for President?**

eighteen (18) and older

*56. **When is the last day you can send in federal income tax forms?**

April 15

*70. **Who was the first President?**

(George) Washington

*75. **What was one important thing that Abraham Lincoln did?**

- freed the slaves (Emancipation Proclamation)
- saved (or preserved) the Union
- led the United States during the Civil War

*78. **Name one war fought by the United States in the 1900s.**

- World War I
- World War II
- Korean War
- Vietnam War
- (Persian) Gulf War

*85. **What did Martin Luther King, Jr. do?**

- fought for civil rights
- worked for equality for all Americans

*94. **What is the capital of the United States?**

Washington, D.C.

*95. **Where is the Statue of Liberty?**

- New York (Harbor)
- Liberty Island

*97. **Why does the flag have 50 stars?**

- because there is one star for each state
- because each star represents a state
- because there are 50 states

*99. **When do we celebrate Independence Day?**

July 4

Civics Practice Quiz: Multiple Choice

At your naturalization interview, you will be asked 6-10 questions from the list of civics questions in the section that began on page 15. You will need to tell the interviewer your answers orally. You will **not** be given a multiple choice test.

However, the multiple choice quiz in the next section gives you another helpful way to practice for the USCIS civics test.

The answers are at the bottom of each page, for easy review. They follow the same order as the USCIS questions that begin on page 15.

Civics Practice Quiz – Multiple Choice

1. What is the "supreme law of the land"?

a. the Supreme Court
b. the President
c. the Declaration of Independence
d. the Constitution

2. What does the Constitution do?

a. sets up the government
b. explains the Declaration of Independence
c. limits immigration
d. describes the nation's freedom from England

3. The idea of self-government is in the first three words of the Constitution. What are these words?

a. Congress shall make
b. We the People
c. We, the colonists
d. All men are created equal

4. What is an amendment?

a. the beginning of the Declaration of Independence
b. the Preamble to the Constitution
c. a change or addition to the Constitution
d. an introduction

5. What do we call the first ten amendments to the Constitution?

a. the Declaration of Independence
b. the Bill of Rights
c. the inalienable rights
d. the Articles of Confederation

Answers: 1 – d, 2 - a, 3 - b, 4 - c, 5 – b

*6. What is one right or freedom in the First Amendment?

a. the right to bear arms
b. the right to vote
c. the right to free speech
d. the right to trial by jury

7. How many amendments does the Constitution have?

a. 10
b. 15
c. 22
d. 27

8. What did the Declaration of Independence say?

a. that all Americans are independent from the government
b. that the British colonists in North America were creating their own independent country
c that colonial America was independent from Canada
d. that American was independent from France

9. What are two rights in the Declaration of Independence?

a. the right to happiness and a good job
b. liberty and an independent government
c. liberty and the pursuit of happiness
d. wealth and good health

10. What is freedom of religion?

a. You must choose a religion.
b. You can have any religion you want or not have a religion.
c. You can choose the time you observe your religion.
d. You do not need to pay to join a church or temple.

Answers: 6 - c, 7 - d, 8 - b, 9 - c, 10 - b

*11. **What is the economic system of the United States?**

a. socialism
b. capitalism
c. democracy
d. communism

12. **What is the rule of law?**

a. Everyone must follow the law.
b. Everyone but the President must follow the law.
c. The president makes the laws.
d. All laws must be the same in every state.

*13. **Name one branch of government.**

a. the Supreme Court
b state government
c. the House of Representatives
d. the executive

14. **What stops any one branch of government from becoming too powerful?**

a. the power of the presidency
b. the voters
c. checks and balances
d. freedom of speech

15. **Who is in charge of the executive branch?**

a. the President
b. the Secretary of Defense
c. the Vice President
d. the Congress

Answers: 11 – b, 12 – a, 13 – d, 14 – c, 15 – a

16. Who makes federal laws?

a. the Supreme Court
b. the President
c. Congress
d. the states

*17. What are the two parts to the U.S. Congress?

a. the Supreme Court and the lower courts
b. the Senate and all the state governors
c. the House of Lords and the House of Commons
d. the Senate and House of Representatives

18. How many U.S. senators are there in the Senate?

a. 50
b. 2
c. 100
d. 200

19. How many years is a senator elected for each term?

a. ten (10)
b. six (6)
c. four (4)
d. two (2)

*20. Who is one of your state's two U.S. senators?

_____

Answers: 16 - c, 17 - d, 18 - c, 19 - b, 20 your answer-- check **www.usa.gov** or ask a librarian

21. How many voting members does the House of Representatives have?

a. 100
b. 200
c. 435
d. 365

22. We elect a U.S. representative for how many years?

a. eight (8)
b. four (4)
c. two (2)
d. six (6)

23. Name your representative.

_____

24. Who does a U.S. senator represent?

a. the state legislatures
b. all the people of his state
c. only the people in the state who voted for the senator
d. all the people of the state who belong to the senator's political party

25. Why do some states have more representatives than others?

a. larger states get more representatives.
b. the number of representatives is based on the population in the state.
c. states that have been part of the U.S. longer have more representatives.
d. small states do not have many representatives.

Answers: 21 - c; 22 – c; 23 your representative — check *www.usa.gov* or call your local library; 24 - b, 25 - b

26. How many years does a President serve in one term?

a. eight (8)
b. two (2)
c. six (6)
d. four (4)

*27. In what month do we elect a president?

a. July
b. November
c. January
d. October

*28. Who is President of the United States now?

a. Mike Pence
b. Barack Obama
c. Donald Trump
d. Franklin Roosevelt

29. Who is Vice President now?

a. Mike Pence
b. Hillary Clinton
c. Barack Obama
d. Thomas Jefferson

30. If the President can no longer serve, who becomes President?

a. the President Pro-Tempore
b. the Secretary of State
c. the Vice President
d. the President

Answers: 26 - d, 27 - b, 28 - c, 29 - a, 30 - c

31. If the President and Vice President can no longer serve, who becomes President?

a. the Speaker of the House
b. the Secretary of State
c. the Vice President
d. the Secretary of Defense

32. Who is the Commander in Chief of the military?

a. the Vice President
b. the President
c. General Pershing
d. the Secretary of Defense

33. Who signs the bills from Congress to make them into laws?

a. the President of the Senate
b. the vice President
c. the Speaker of the House
d. the President

34. Who can veto bills from Congress?

a. the Vice President
b. the President
c. the Speaker of the House
d. the President Pro Tempore

35. What does the President's Cabinet do?

a. writes the yearly budget to submit to Congress
b. approves presidential appointments
c. advises the President
d. works closely with Congress

Answers: 31 - a, 32 - b, 33 - d, 34 - b, 35 - c

36. Which of the following are two Cabinet-level positions?

a. Secretary of State and Secretary of the Treasury
b. Secretary of Health and Human Services and Secretary of the Navy
c. Secretary of Weather and Secretary of Energy
d. Secretary of the Interior and Secretary of History

37. What does the judicial branch of government do?

a. reviews and explains laws
b. appoints judges
c. makes laws
d. chooses Supreme Court judges

38. What is the highest court in the country?

a. the Appeals Court
b. the Supreme Court
c. superior courts
d. district courts

39. How many justices are on the Supreme Court?

a. eleven (11)
b. ten (10)
c. nine (9)
d. twelve (12)

40 . Who is the Chief Justice of the United States now?

a. Barack Obama
b. Donald Trump
c. Anthony Kennedy
d. John Roberts

Answers: 36 - a, 37 - a, 38 - b, 39 - c, 40 - d

41. Under our Constitution, some powers belong to the federal government. What is one power of the federal government?

a. to make treaties with foreign governments
b. to set up police departments
c. to build all schools
d. to issue driver's licenses

42. The Constitution gives powers to the states. Which of the following is not a state power?

a to issue driver's licenses
b. to collect taxes
c. to print money
d. to provide safety for the public (police and fire departments)

43. Who is the governor of your state?

_____

*44. What is your state capital?

_____

*45. What are the two major political parties in the United States today?

a. American and Bull-Moose
b. Democratic and Republican
c. Democratic-Republican and Whigs
d. Libertarian and Green

Answers; 41 - a, 42 - c, 43 - check **www.usa.gov** for your state's governor; 44 – see p.25; 45 - b

46. What is the political party of the President now?

a. Democratic Party
b. Independent Party
c. Green Party
d. Republican Party

47. What is the name of the current Speaker of the House?

a. Barack Obama
b. Kamala Harris
c. Nancy Pelosi
d. Mitch McConnell

48. There are four amendments to the Constitution about voting. Describe one of them.

a. Only citizens by birth can vote.
b. Only citizens older than 21 can vote.
c. Citizens eighteen (18) and older can vote.
d. Only citizens with a job can vote.

*49. Which of the following is not a responsibility for all U.S. citizens?

a. serve on a jury
b. get a passport
c. vote
d. pay taxes

50. Which of the following rights is only for U.S. citizens?

a. to pay taxes
b. to go to college
c. to get medical care
d. to vote

Answers: 46 - d, 47 - c, 48 - c, 49 - b, 50 - d

51. Which two rights are for citizens and non-citizens living in the U.S.?

a. freedom of speech and the right to vote
b. freedom of speech and serving on a jury
c. freedom of speech and freedom of religion
d. the right to vote and the right to travel with a U.S. passport

52. What do we show loyalty to when we say the Pledge of Allegiance?

a. the Founding Fathers
b. the United States
c. the Constitution
d. the U.S. military

53. What is one promise that you make when you become a U.S. citizen?

a. to bring your family to the United States
b. to get a driver's license
c. to be loyal to the United States
d. to get an American passport

*54. How old are U.S. citizens when they can begin to vote?

a. 21
b. 18
c. 25
d. 20

55. What are two ways that Americans can participate in their democracy?

a. vote and join a civic group
b. give an elected official your opinion on an issue and vote
c. write to a newspaper and call their congressmen
d. all of these answers

Answers: 51 - c, 52 - b, 53 - c, 54 - b, 55 - d

*56. When is the last day you can send in federal income tax forms?

a. July 4
b. April 15
c. May 15
d. March 15

57. When must all men register for the Selective Service?

a. between eighteen (18) and twenty-six (26)
b. at any age
c. only at age eighteen (18)
d. American men do not have to register

58. Why did colonists come to America?

a. for religious freedom
b. for political freedom
c. for economic opportunities
d. all of the above

59. Who lived in America before the Europeans arrived?

a. no one
b. Floridians
c. American Indians
d. Canadians

60. What group of people was captured and taken to America then sold as slaves?

a. English settlers
b. Canadians
c. Dutch
d. Africans

Answers: 56 - b, 57 - a, 58 - d, 59 - c, 60 - d

61. Why did the colonists fight the British?

a. because they didn't have self-government
b. because of unfair taxes
c. because the British army stayed in the colonists homes
d. all of these answers

62. Who wrote the Declaration of Independence?

a. George Washington
b. Thomas Jefferson
c. Benjamin Franklin
d. James Madison

63. When was the Declaration of Independence adopted?

a. July 4, 1776
b. January 1, 1775
c. December 10, 1776
d. July 1, 1775

64. There were 13 original states. Which of the following were included?

a. Georgia, Maine, Texas
b. New Hampshire, New York, New Mexico
c. Georgia, Pennsylvania, New York
d. Rhode Island, Delaware, Washington

65. What happened at the Constitutional Convention?

a. The Constitution was presented to King George
b. The Constitution was written
c. They wrote the Bill of Rights
d. They wrote the Declaration of Independence

Answers: 61 - d, 62 - b, 63 - a, 64 - c, 65 - b

66. When was the Constitution written?

a. 1776
b. 1787
c. 1789
d. 1790

67. The Federalist Papers supported the passage of the U.S. Constitution. Name one writer.

a. John Adams
b. George Washington
c. James Madison
d. Thomas Jefferson

68. What is one thing Benjamin Franklin is famous for?

a. He was the youngest member of the Constitutional Convention.
b. He was third President of the United States.
c. He was a writer and diplomat.
d. all of the above

69. Who is "The Father of Our Country"?

a. George Washington
b. Barack Obama
c. John F. Kennedy
d. Abraham Lincoln

*70. Who was the first president of the United States?

a. Thomas Jefferson
b. George Washington
c. James Madison
d. John Adams

Answers: 66 - b, 67 - c, 68 - c, 69 - a, 70 - b

71. What territory did the United States buy from France in 1803?

a. Quebec
b. Haiti
c. Louisiana
d. Alaska

72. Name one war fought by the U.S. in the 1800s (the nineteenth century).

a. World War II
b. Civil War
c. Korean War
d. World War I

73. Name the U.S. war between the northern and southern states.

a. the American Revolution
b. the Civil War
c. the War of 1812
d. the Vietnam War

74. Which of these problems led to the Civil War?

a. slavery
b. economic conflicts
c. international treaties
d. a and b

*75. What was one important thing that Abraham Lincoln did?

a. established the United Nations
b. lead the U.S. to victory in World War I
c. saved (or preserved) the Union
d. purchased Alaska for the United States

Answers: 71 - c, 72 - b, 73 - b, 74 - d, 75 - c

76. What did the Emancipation Proclamation do?

a. freed the slaves
b. gave women the right to vote
c. ended the Civl War
d. ended World War I

77. Which of the following women fought for women's right to vote?

a. Emily Dickinson
b. Martha Washington
c. Susan B. Anthony
d. Dolley Madison

*78. Name one war fought by the U.S. in the 1900s (the twentieth century).

a. the French-Indian War
b. the Korean War
c. the Spanish-American War
d. the Mexican-American War

79. Who was President during World War I?

a. Theodore Roosevelt
b. Franklin Roosevelt
c. Woodrow Wilson
d. Warren Harding

80. Who was President during World War II?

a. Theodore Roosevelt
b. Franklin Roosevelt
c. Woodrow Wilson
d. Warren Harding

Answers: 76 - a, 77 - c, 78 - b, 79 - c, 80 - b

81. Who did the U.S. fight in WWII?

a. Japan
b. Germany
c. Italy
d. all of the above

82. Before he was President, Eisenhower was a general. Which war was he in?

a. Civil War
b. World War II
c. Spanish-American War
d. Vietnam War

83. During the Cold War, what was the main concern of the United States?

a. the Great Depression
b. climate change
c. communism
d. slavery

84. What movement tried to end racial discrimination?

a. civil rights movement
b. conservation
c. prohibition
d. women's suffrage

*85. What did Dr. Martin Luther King, Jr. do?

a. wrote the Declaration of Independence
b. ended slavery
c. led peaceful protests for civil rights
d. was the first African-American Secretary of State

Answers: 81 - d, 82 - b, 83 - c, 84 - a, 85 - c

86. What major event happened on September 11, 2001 in the United States?

a. Hurricane Andrew struck the southern United States
b. There was a nuclear accident at Three-Mile Island
c. Terrorists attacked the United States
d. The Japanese attacked Pearl Harbor

87. Which of the following is not an American Indian (Native American) tribe?

a. Cherokee
b. Celts
c. Crow
d. Apache

88. Which of the following is the longest river in the United States?

a. the Columbia River
b. the Missouri River
c. the Colorado River
d. the Hudson River

89. Which ocean is on the West Coast of the United States?

a. Pacific Ocean
b. Arctic Ocean
c. Indian Ocean
d. Atlantic Ocean

90. What ocean is on the East Coast of the United States?

a. Pacific Ocean
b. Arctic Ocean
c. Indian Ocean
d. Atlantic Ocean

Answers: 86 - c, 87 - b, 88 - b, 89 - a, 90 - d

91. Which of the following is not a U.S. territory?

a. American Samoa
b. Okinawa
c. Puerto Rico
d. Guam

92. Name one state that borders Canada.

a. Rhode Island
b. South Dakota
c. Maine
d. Oregon

93. Which state borders Mexico?

a. Kansas
b. Texas
c. Utah
d. Washington

*94. What is the capitol city of the U.S.?

a. New York City, NY.
b. Washington, D.C.
c. Hollywood, California
d. Boston, Massachusetts

*95. Where is the Statue of Liberty?

a. Long Island
b. New York Harbor
c. San Francisco Bay
d. Boston Harbor

Answers: 91 - b, 92 - c, 93 - b, 94 - b, 95 - b

96. Why does the flag have 13 stripes?

a. because the stripes represent the 13 members of the `` Second Continental Congress
b. because it was good luck to have 13 stripes on a flag
c. because the stripes represent the original 13 colonies
d. because there were 13 signatures on the Declaration of Independence

*97. Why does the flag have 50 stars?

a. for the 50 original Founding Fathers of America
b. for the 50 states
c. for the original 50 colonies
d. for the 50 departments in the federal government

98. What is the U.S. national anthem?

a. "Stars and Stripes Forever"
b. "America, the Beautiful"
c. "The Star-Spangled Banner"
d. "Grand Old Flag"

*99. When do we celebrate Independence Day?

a. July 4
b. January 1
c. October 31
d. April 15

100. Which of the following are not two official national holidays?

a. Christmas and Thanksgiving
b. Presidents' Day and Columbus Day
c. Veteran's Day and Memorial Day
d. Valentine's Day and Halloween

Answers: 96 - c, 97 - b, 98 - c, 99 - a, 100 - d

Reading Vocabulary — USCIS

Reading Vocabulary
USCIS Recommended List

At your naturalization interview, the USCIS officer will show you 1-3 sentences in English. You must read one (1) of these three (3) sentences correctly to show that you can read English. The following list shows the words that USCIS recommends that you should know. You will not know the sentences that USCIS will ask you to read until you take the test.

Question Words	Other
how	a
what	for
when	here
where	in
why	of
who	on
	the
	to
	we

Verbs	Other
can	colors
come	dollar bill
do/does	first
elects	largest
have/has	many
be/is/are/was	most
lives/lived	north
meet	one
name	people
pay	second
vote	south
want	

People

George Washington
Abraham Lincoln

Civics

American flag
Bill of Rights
capital
citizen
city
Congress
country
Father of Our Country
government
President
right
Senators
state/states
White House

Places

America
United States
U.S.

Holidays

Presidents' Day
Memorial Day
Flag Day
Independence Day
Labor Day
Columbus Day
Thanksgiving

Writing Vocabulary — USCIS

Practice tip: Have someone read short sentences to you using these vocabulary words. Practice writing the sentences as they are dictated (spoken) to you.

Writing Vocabulary
USCIS Recommended List

The following list shows the words that USCIS recommends that you know for the writing test. The USCIS officer will read 1-3 sentences to you. You must write one (1) of these three (3) sentences correctly to show that you can write in English. You will not know the sentences that USCIS will use until you take the test.

Months

February
September
May
October
June
November
July

People

Adams
Lincoln
Washington

Civics

American Indian
capital
citizens
Civil War
Congress
Father of Our Country
flag
free
freedom of speech
President
right
Senators
state/states
White House

Holidays

Presidents' Day
Columbus Day
Thanksgiving
Flag Day

Labor Day
Memorial Day
Independence Day

Places

Alaska
California
Canada
Delaware
Mexico
New York City
Washington, D.C.
United States

Verbs

be/is/was
can
come
elect
have/has
lives/lived
meets
pay
vote
want

Other (content)

blue
dollar bill
fifty / 50
first
largest
most
north
one

Other

one hundred / 100
people
red
second
south
taxes
white

Other (Function)

and
during
for
here
in

of
on
the
to
we

You can use the space below to practice writing any difficult words separately or in your own sentences.

★Remember: Every sentence begins with a capital letter. Every sentence ends with a period. Every question ends with a question mark.

★Remember: Capitalize words correctly. The first letter in a sentence is always capitalized. So are names of people. Pay attention to the places and things that are capitalized in the USCIS lists above.

★**Example of a sentence. Be sure to begin with a capital letter and end with a period.**

George Washington was the first president of the United States of America.

★**Example of a question. Be sure to begin with a capital letter and end with a question mark.**

What are the colors of the American flag?

Use the lines below to practice writing difficult vocabulary and writing your own sentences.

_____

_____

_____

_____

_____

_____

For More Information
Helpful U.S. Government Addresses, Websites, and Phone Numbers

For More Information
Helpful U.S. Government Addresses,
Websites, and Phone Numbers

FEDERAL DEPARTMENTS AND AGENCIES

If you don't know where to begin, call: 1-800-FED-INFO (or 1-800-333-4636) for more information. If you are hard-of-hearing, call 1-800-326-2996. The government also has a citizenship website: **http://www.USA.gov.** Look there for general information about government agencies. For forms and other citizenship information, you can also go to the USCIS website at: **www.uscis.gov.** A U.S. government website will end in ".gov".

Department of Education (ED)

U.S. Department of Education
400 Maryland Avenue SW
Washington, DC 20202
Phone: 1-800-872-5327
For hearing impaired: 1-800-437-0833
http://www.ed.gov

Department of Health and Human Services (HHS)

U.S. Department of Health and Human Services
200 Independence Avenue SW
Washington, DC 20201
Phone: 1-877-696-6775
http://www.hhs.gov

Department of Homeland Security (DHS)

U.S. Department of Homeland Security
Washington, DC 20528
http://www.dhs.gov

Department of Housing and Urban Development (HUD)

U.S. Department of Housing and Urban Development
451 7th Street SW
Washington, DC 20410
Phone: 202-708-1112
For hearing impaired: 202-708-1455
http://www.hud.gov

Department of Justice (DOJ)

U.S. Department of Justice
950 Pennsylvania Avenue NW
Washington, DC 20530-0001
Phone: 202-514-2000
http://www.usdoj.gov

Department of State (DOS)

U.S. Department of State
2201 C Street NW
Washington, DC 20520
Phone: 202-647-4000
http://www.state.gov

Equal Employment Opportunity Commission (EEOC)

U.S. Equal Employment Opportunity Commission
1801 L Street NW
Washington, DC 20507
Phone: 1-800-669-4000
For hearing impaired: 1-800-669-6820
http://www.eeoc.gov

Internal Revenue Service (IRS)

Phone: 1-800-829-1040
For hearing impaired: 1-800-829-4059
http://www.irs.gov

Selective Service System (SSS)

Registration Information Office
PO Box 94638
Palatine, IL 60094-4638
Phone: 847-688-6888
http://www.sss.gov

Social Security Administration (SSA)

Office of Public Inquiries
6401 Security Boulevard
Baltimore, MD 21235
Phone: 1-800-772-1213
For hearing impaired: 1-800-325-0778
http://www.socialsecurity.gov or
http://www.segurosocial.gov/espanol/.

U.S. Citizenship and Immigration Services (USCIS)

Phone: 1-800-375-5283
For hearing impaired: 1-800-767-1833
http://www.uscis.gov

U.S. Customs and Border Protection (CBP)

Phone: 202-354-1000
http://www.cbp.gov

U.S. Immigration and Customs Enforcement (ICE)

http://www.ice.gov

Flashcards

100 Civics Questions
Flashcard Format

Directions:

You can make your own flashcards by cutting the paper in this section as directed. (The questions are on the front. The answers are on the back). Then use them to study, practice and review the civics questions.

1. Remove the next pages from this book. Tear and trim or you can remove them with an exacto knife.

2. Cut each page on the dotted lines   --------✂-------
so that you have four separate questions/answers from each page.

3. You can keep these flashcards in an envelope.

4. Practice. Read the question on the front and give the answer. Then look at the back to see if your answer was correct.

front

What is the supreme law of the land?

back

The Constitution

5. Keep the questions that you miss in a separate group from the questions that you already know the answers to. Practice the ones you don't know again and again.

1. What is the supreme (highest) law of the land?

-------- ✂ --------

2. What does the Constitution do?

-------- ✂ --------

3. The idea of self-government is in the first three words of the Constitution. What are these words?

-------- ✂ --------

4. What is an amendment?

1. the Constitution

2. It sets up the government

   You need to know one answer.
   For more choices, see page 15.

3. We the People

4. a change to the Constitution

5. What do we call the first ten amendments to the Constitution?

- -

*6. What is one right or freedom in the First Amendment?

- -

7. How many amendments does the Constitution have?

- -

8. What did the Declaration of Independence do?

5. the Bill of Rights

*6. freedom of religion

   You need to know one answer for USCIS.
   For other correct answers, see page 16.

7. Twenty-seven (27)

8. It announced our independence (from Great Britain).
   You need to know one answer.

   For more choices, see page 16.

9. What are two rights in the Declaration of Independence?

----

10. What is freedom of religion?

----

*11. What is the economic system in the United States?

----

12. What is the "rule of law"?

9. – life
    - liberty

    You need to know two rights.
    For more choices, see page 17.

10. People can observe (have) any
    religion or no religion

*11. capitalist economy

12. Everyone must follow the law.

    You need to know one answer.
    For other choices, see page 17.

*13. Name one branch or part of
      the government.

----

14. What stops one branch of government
     from becoming too powerful?

----

15. Who is in charge of the
     executive branch?

----

16. Who makes federal laws?

*13. the legislative branch. (Congress)

You need to know one branch.
For other choices, see page 18.

14. checks and balances

15. the President

16. Congress

* 17. What are the two parts of
      the U.S. Congress?

----

18. How many U.S. senators are
    here in the Senate?

----

19. We elect a U.S. senator for how
    many years per term?

----

*20. Who is one of your state's
     U.S. senators now?

*17. the Senate and House of Representatives

18. one hundred (100)

19. six (6)

*20. My senator is _____ If you
       don't know who it is, go online to www.senate.gov.

       [Residents of the District of Columbia or U.S.
       territories should say that they have no U.S.
       senators.]

21. How many members does the House of Representatives have?

----

22. We elect a U.S. representative for how many years per term?

----

23. Name your U.S. representative.

----

24. Who does a U.S. senator represent?

21. four hundred thirty-five (435)

22. two (2)

23. My representative is _____
    Answers will depend on where you live. If you don't
    know who your representative is, go online to
    www.usa.gov or ask at your local library.

    [If you live in a territory, not a state, you can say
    that "the territory has no voting representatives in
    Congress."]

24. All the people of his or her state.

25. Why do some states have more
    representatives than other states?

----

26. We elect a President for how many
    years per term?

----

*27. In what month do we vote
     for President?

----

*28. What is the name of the President of
     the United States now?

25. Because they have more people in their state.

You need to know one correct answer.
For other choices, see page 20.

26. four (4)

*27. November

*28. Donald Trump

For another way to say this, see page 21.

29. What is the name of the Vice President of the United States now?

- -

30. If the President can no longer serve, who becomes President?

- -

31. If both the President and the Vice President can no longer serve, who becomes President?

- -

32. Who is the Commander in Chief of the military?

29. Mike Pence

For another way to say this,
see page 21.

30. the Vice President

31. the Speaker of the House

32. the President

33. Who signs bills so they become laws?

- -

34. Who can veto bills?

- -

35. What does the President's
Cabinet do?

- -

36. What are two Cabinet-level
positions?

33. the President

34. the President

35. It advises the President.

36. Vice President;
Secretary of State

You only need to know 2 positions.
For other choices, see page 23.

37. What does the judicial branch do?

----

38. What is the highest court in
    the United States?

----

39. How many justices are on the
    Supreme Court?

----

40. Who is the Chief Justice of
    the United States now?

37. It explains laws.

You need to know one answer.
For other choices, see page 23.

38. the Supreme Court

39. nine (9)

40. John Roberts

41. Under our Constitution, some powers belong to the federal government What is <u>one</u> power of the federal government?

- -

42. Under our Constitution, some powers belong to the states. What is <u>one</u> power of the states?

- -

43. Who is the governor of your state now?

- -

*44. What is the capital of your state?

41. to declare war

You need to know one power.
For other choices, see page 24.

42. to give a driver's license

You only need to know one power.
For more choices, see page 24.

43. My governor is _____

Answers will depend on the state you live in. If you don't
know, ask at your local library or go to www.usa.gov.

[If you live in the District of Columbia you should
answer that D.C. does not have a governor.]

*44. The capital is _____
See page 25 for the list of state capitals.

[District of Columbia residents should answer that D.C.
is not a state and does not have a capital. Residents of
U.S. territories should name the territory's capital.]

*45. What are the two major political
parties in the United States?

----

46. What is the political party
of the President now?

----

47. What is the name of the Speaker of
the House of Representatives?

----

48. There are four amendments to the
Constitution about who can vote.
Describe one of them.

*45.   the Democratic Party and
       the Republican Party

46.   the Republican Party

47.   Nancy Pelosi

48.   Any U.S. citizen over 18 years old
      can vote.

      You need to know one amendment.
      For other choices, see page 27.

*49. What is one responsibility that is only
     for United States citizens?

----

50. Name one right only for United States
    citizens.

----

51. What are two rights of everyone living in
    the United States?

----

52. What do we show loyalty to when we
    say the Pledge of Allegiance?

*49. to serve on a jury

You only need to know one answer.
For other choices, see page 27.

50. to vote in a U.S. election

51. Freedom of speech.
The right to a trial by jury.

For more choices, see page 27.

52. the United States

53. What is one promise you make when
    you become a United States citizen?

----

*54. How old do citizens have to be to vote
    for President?

----

55. What are two ways that Americans can
    participate in their democracy?

----

*56. When is the last day you can send in
    federal income tax forms?

53. to defend the U.S.

    You need to know one answer.
    For more choices, see page 28.

*54. At least 18 years old (eighteen and older)

55. (1) vote;
    (2) join a political party

    For more choices, see page 28.

*56. April 15

57. When must all men register for the Selective Service?

----

58. What is one reason colonists came to America?

----

59. Who lived in America before the Europeans arrived?

----

60. What group of people was taken to America by force and sold as slaves?

57. at age eighteen (18)

58. for freedom

You need to know one reason.
For more reasons, see page 29.

59. American Indians

For another way to say it, see page 30.

60. people from Africa

61. Why did the colonists fight the British?
    (Know one reason.)

- -

62. Who wrote the Declaration of Independence?

- -

63. When was the Declaration of Independence
    adopted?

- -

64. There were 13 original states.
    Name three.

61. because of high taxes
    ("taxation without representation")

    You need to know one answer.
    For other choices, see page 30.

62. Thomas Jefferson

63. July 4, 1776

64. New York
    New Jersey
    North Carolina

    For a complete list, see page 31.

65. What happened at the Constitutional Convention ?
    (Know one way to say it.)

----

66. When was the Constitution written?

----

67. The Federalist Papers supported the passage of the U.S. Constitution. Name one of the writers.

----

68. What is one thing Benjamin Franklin is famous for?

65. The Constitution was written.

66. 1787

67. (James) Madison

You need to know one writer.
For other choices, see page 31.

68. He started the first free libraries

You need to know one answer.
For more choices, see page 32.

69. Who is the "Father of Our Country"?

----

*70. Who was the first President?

----

71. What territory did the United States buy from France in 1803?

----

72. Name one war fought by the United States in the 1800s.

69. (George) Washington

*70. (George) Washington

71. Louisiana

   For another way to say this,
   see page 32.

72. the Civil War

   You need to know one war.
   For more choices, see page 33.

73. Name the U.S. war between
    the North and the South.

----

74. Name one problem that led to the
    Civil War.

----

*75. What was one important thing that
    Abraham Lincoln did?

----

76. What did the Emancipation
    Proclamation do?

73. the Civil War

For another way to say this, see page 33.

74. slavery

You need to know one answer.
For other choices, see page 33.

*75. He freed the slaves.

You need to know one answer.
For other choices, see page 33.

76. It freed the slaves

You need to know one answer. For
another choice, see page 34.

77. What did Susan B. Anthony do?

----

*78. Name one war fought by the United
     States in the 1900s.

----

79. Who was President during World War I?

----

80. Who was President during the Great
    Depression and World War II?

77. She fought for women's rights

You need to know one answer. For another choice, see page 34.

*78. World War I

You need to know one answer. For more choices, see page 34.

79. (Woodrow) Wilson

80. Franklin Roosevelt

81. Who did the United States fight
    in World War II?

----

82. Before he was President, Eisenhower
    was a general. What war was he in?

----

83. During the Cold War, what was the
    main concern of the United States?

----

84. What movement tried to end racial
    discrimination?

81. Japan, Germany, and Italy

82. World War II

83. Communism

84. the civil rights movement

*85. What did Martin Luther King, Jr. do?

----

86. What major event happened on September 11,
     2001, in the United States?

----

87. Name one American Indian tribe in
     the United States.

----

88. Name one of the two longest rivers in
     the United States.

*85. He worked for equality for
all Americans.

You need to know one answer. For
other ways to answer, see page 35.

86. Terrorists attacked the United States.

87. Pueblo

You need to know <u>one</u> tribe.
For more tribes, see page 36.

88. Missouri (River)

You need to know one river.
For the other river, see page 36.

89. What ocean is on the West Coast of the United States?

----

90. What ocean is on the East Coast of the United States?

----

91. Name one U.S. territory.

----

92. Name one state that borders Canada.

89. Pacific (Ocean)

90. Atlantic (Ocean)

91. Puerto Rico

   You need to know one territory.
   To see the complete list, see page 37.

92. Alaska

   You need to know one state.
   To see the complete list, see page 37.

93. Name one state that borders Mexico.

----

*94. What is the capital of the
      United States?

----

*95. Where is the Statue of Liberty?

----

96. Why does the flag have 13 stripes?

93. California

> You need to know one state.
> To see a complete list, see page 37.

*94. Washington, D.C.

*95. New York Harbor

> You need to know one answer.
> For other ways to answer, see page 38.

96. The stripes represent the original 13 colonies.

*97. Why does the flag have 50 stars?

----

98. What is the name of the national anthem?

----

*99. When do we celebrate Independence Day?

----

100. Name two national U.S. holidays.

*97. The stars represent the 50 U.S. states.

For other ways to say this, see page 38.

98. "The Star-Spangled Banner"

*99. July 4

100. - Thanksgiving
  - Christmas

You need to know two holidays.
For the complete list, see page 39.

Made in the USA
San Bernardino, CA
07 September 2019